better together*

*This book is best read together, grownup and kid.

a kids
book
about
TM

a kids book about™ white privilege

by Ben Sand

a kids book about™

Printed in the United States of America

Library of Congress cataloging available.

A Kids Book About books are exclusively available online on the A Kids Book About website.

To share your stories, ask questions, or inquire about bulk purchases (schools, libraries, and nonprofits), please use the following email address:

hello@akidsbookabout.com

www.akidsbookabout.com

ISBN: 978-1-951253-46-2

For Adah, Zoe, and Julin.
Let's use what we've been given
to change the world.

—Dad

Intro

It's time white parents talk to white kids about race.

To be a child in the world today is to be confronted with the complexities of race, but we still have a long way to go when it comes to this conversation, and we've neglected the topic of privilege for too long. So, I decided to write this book with the hope that the white children growing up today will see their privilege and use it for good.

Let's be the parents that decide not to perpetuate the myth that all children start from the same spot. Instead, let's empower our children with the knowledge to build a new space together.

Hi, my name is Ben,
and this is my book about
white privilege.

White privilege? What's that?!

Well, first, I have to explain to you what I mean by "white."

I want you to look at the color of your skin.

What color is it?

When I look at my arm, it's kind of pinkish, reddish, beige.

Like the color of this page.

But when people talk about what color I am, they would say "white."

But why?

If white is actually the color of this page and my skin looks different, then what does it mean that I'm white?

Well, grownups a long time ago decided to create labels for people.

These labels
were determined
by skin color.*

*There's a long and complicated reason for this
but we don't have time to get into it.

Some of these labels were

,

Black,

brown,

etc.

Okay, now we need to talk about the other word: privilege

Privilege is when someone
has an advantage they
haven't earned.

Like when your classmate is always chosen to be team captain just because their mom is the coach.

Or when you're racing your friend, but they get a head start.

So
then
what
is

white pr

ivilege?

White privilege is when people who are white have additional benefits, advantages, and fewer barriers to overcome than people of color.*

*People of color are folks with black or brown skin or of a specific race or ethnicity.

That doesn't mean that if you're white, you aren't talented, or smart, or your life is easy.

It means you have extra privileges just because of the color of your skin.

Really?!
Yes, really.

So, what are some of those privileges?

Sometimes they're...

small.

and sometimes they're...

REALLY BIG

Like the privilege of always seeing people who look like you in books and movies.

That might seem like
no big deal, but imagine if
no one looked like you in
your favorite movie.

Wouldn't that make you
feel left out or sad?

Or it can be in the people who are usually in charge, like teachers, your parent's boss, and presidents.

Those people are
usually white.

This is probably something you've never really thought about.

That's okay.

But don't you wonder why those people are often white and not another color?

White privilege could
also be in the things you
don't have to worry about...

that people of color do.

Like...

Feeling unsafe when you walk past a police officer.

Having people assume you're bad at something because of your skin color.

Easily finding a Band-Aid that matches your skin tone.

Or people always asking you where you're REALLY from.

These are just some of the ways that white privilege can show up without anyone noticing.

In fact, part of having white privilege can mean that you don't even know you have it.

The thing about white privilege is that you don't have to think about being white.

This was also true of me.

As a kid, I never thought about being white. I never thought that I had extra privileges. But because of my white privilege...

Strangers smiled at me when I walked down the street.

I would get invited to more places and parties.

I felt safe when out and about.

I had more opportunities.

People didn't look down on me.

And I had a better shot at success.

I had all these advantages, even though I grew up without a dad, no money, and never really knew what tomorrow would look like.

Having white privilege
doesn't mean that everything
about my life is perfect or better
than a person of color.

It means that I had a head start.

I didn't earn that head start.

I didn't ask for that head start.

But I had a head start.

Because I was white.

But here's the thing,

I could feel guilty about
my white privilege.

(Which I did, for a while.)

But what good would that do?
Who would that help?

It doesn't make me a bad person
to have white privilege.

But I can't pretend that
it doesn't exist.

So instead of feeling guilty,
I realized I needed to:

See it.

It was up to me to accept that my privilege was there and learn more about it and how it affects the people around me—especially people of color.

Use it for good.

I also learned that I could use my privilege for good! You can too! Commit to listening to people of color, learning from them, and helping others without your privilege, which sometimes means stepping back and letting them take the lead.

Give
it up.

Since I didn't earn my privilege, it's not really mine, but I have the power to give it up. When it puts me at the front of the line, when it gets in the way of someone else, or when it can lift someone else up.

It's not always clear how to do this, but it's important to try.

When we do these things, we shouldn't expect an award for it.

It's just...

THE RIGHT THING TO DO.

Seeing your white privilege isn't easy. It took me a long time.

Using it for good and giving
it up is even harder.

But if you're white and you're reading this book, I just want to say...

Understanding and acknowledging your white privilege is not just important, it's **your responsibility**.

Have the courage to ask the question: What privileges do I have because I'm white?

Then have

EVEN
MORE
COUI

RAGE
to find out the answers!

Outro

Phew. We did it! You just talked with your kid about white privilege. Hopefully, this book surfaces a desire to keep the conversation going.

Seize this moment!

Here are a few questions you might ask your kid as you discern how these ideas translate into a healthy identity and appropriate action:

1. How do you feel after learning about white privilege?

2. Do you have any questions about how white people experience the world differently than people of color?

3. What should we do to understand our privilege and use it for good?

find
more
kids
books
about

systemic racism, emotions, gender, autism, community, adoption, belonging, shame, empathy, gratitude, and mindfulness.

■ **akidsbookabout.com**

share your read*

*Tell somebody, post a photo, or give this book away to share what you care about.

@akidsbookabout